GOOD NIGHT, LITTLE BUG

Written by Cynthia Rothman
Illustrated by Maj-Britt Hagsted

"Just one more run," said the bug.

"Just one more run," said her mother.

"Just one more hug," said her mother.

"No," said her mother.

And the little bug went to sleep, snug as a bug in a rug.

8